HAL•LEONARD
INSTRUMENTAL
PLAY-ALONG

AUDIO
ACCESS
INCLUDED

PLAYBACK+
eed • Pitch • Balance • Loop

VIOLA

CHRISTMAS CLASSICS

Audio arrangements by Peter Deneff

To access audio visit:
www.halleonard.com/mylibrary

Enter Code
5518-1231-8030-6910

ISBN 978-1-4950-7062-4

HAL•LEONARD®
CORPORATION
7777 W. BLUEMOUND RD. P.O. BOX 13819 MILWAUKEE, WI 53213

In Australia Contact:
Hal Leonard Australia Pty. Ltd.
4 Lentara Court
Cheltenham, Victoria, 3192 Australia
Email: ausadmin@halleonard.com.au

Visit Hal Leonard Online at
www.halleonard.com

ANGELS WE HAVE HEARD ON HIGH

VIOLA

Traditional French Carol

BRING A TORCH, JEANNETTE, ISABELLA

VIOLA

17th Century French Provençal Carol

COVENTRY CAROL

VIOLA

Traditional English Melody

FUM, FUM, FUM

VIOLA

Traditional Catalonian Carol

GO, TELL IT ON THE MOUNTAIN

VIOLA

African-American Spiritual

GOD REST YE MERRY, GENTLEMEN

VIOLA

Traditional English Carol

HERE WE COME A-CAROLING

VIOLA

Traditional

THE HOLLY AND THE IVY

VIOLA

18th Century English Carol

I SAW THREE SHIPS

VIOLA

Traditional English Carol

JINGLE BELLS

Words and Music by
J. PIERPONT

VIOLA

O COME, ALL YE FAITHFUL

VIOLA

Music by JOHN FRANCIS WADE

O HOLY NIGHT

VIOLA

French Words by PLACIDE CAPPEAU
English Words by JOHN S. DWIGHT
Music by ADOLPHE ADAM

SILENT NIGHT

VIOLA

Words by JOSEPH MOHR
Music by FRANZ X. GRUBER

STILL, STILL, STILL

VIOLA

Salzburg Melody, c.1819

WHAT CHILD IS THIS?

VIOLA

16th Century English Melody